Design It

Edition 2

Contents

BY ROGER COOK

ILLUSTRATED BY SERENA KEARNS

Sk8r Jam Apparel

Ever since you can remember, you've had a dream about starting your own T-shirt design business, and now it seems the dream is about to become a reality. With luck, that creative, entrepreneurial spirit you were born with is finally going to earn you some money.

For three years, it's been nothing but sweat equity—researching other small businesses and their company stationery, dreaming up logos, exploring different T-shirt designs, and packaging ideas. You've worked hard at the supermarket packing groceries, pushing every single shopping cart there ever was. You've done odd jobs here, there, and everywhere, washing cars in the neighborhood until you're positive your fingerprints have been permanently washed off!

The "sound advice" you got from your parents about starting your own business has finally paid off, and the dollars have slowly begun piling up. Your parents even helped you with your business plan.

Now the day has arrived at last. It's your first step toward financial independence. You're ready to start your own small business—Sk8r Jam Apparel.

CLOSE READING

Why does the author begin the text by addressing "you"? What effect does this technique have on you as a reader?

CLOSE READING

Why do you think the steps in the SK8R Jam Apparel business plan are given in this order?

To Do List

	Job for me	Job for outsourcing
– design logo	x	
– business cards		
design	x	
printing	x	
– design and stencil T-shirt	x	?
print more T-shirts		?
– design packaging	x	
– decorate packaging???	x	
– clothing tags		

other stuff?

Business Plan

- SK8R JAM APPAREL

Simple Business Plan Outline

1. Executive summary—objectives, mission, etc.
2. Description of company—about the company and rough start-up expenses
3. Company product or services—types of t-shirts, sourcing, and buying
4. Market analysis—market potential, market competition
5. Strategy and implementation—marketing strategy, sales strategy
6. Financial plan—profit and loss plan, cash flow plan
7. Future—Web site, e-marketing, etc.

The Basics of Logo Design

Before you start your logo, research, research, research! You need to understand what a logo is, what it represents, and what it is supposed to do.

Your logo is not just a mark—it needs to reflect your business's commercial brand. You can achieve this through the use of shapes, symbols, text, color, and images.

What type of logo are you after?

- text logo
- shape/symbol logo
- text AND shape/symbol logo

Some of the Dos and Don'ts of Logo Design

1. Keep your logo simple. This makes it easily legible.
2. Make your logo timeless and unique.
3. Choose fonts that best reflect your business and read well on business cards and posters.
4. Design your logo in such a way that it will look good no matter what its size, color, or application.
5. Don't use too many colors. The more colors you use, the more difficult and expensive it will be to reproduce.
6. Avoid using shading or gradients of color in your logo.
7. Try to use vector computer graphics in your logo, rather than raster graphics.
8. Don't plagiarize other people's ideas. It is NOT COOL, and it's illegal.
9. Think ahead. You may want to apply your logo to other media in the future.

It is imperative that your logo is well thought out and well designed. There is good and bad design when it comes to logos. Great logo design can literally **make** or **break** your business.

Here are a few reasons why you need a good logo.

- to brand your business
- to make your business more memorable
- to explain your business name
- to differentiate your business from your competition
- to show your commitment
- to attract more clients
- to give the illusion that your business is "bigger" and more "established"

Once you feel you've done enough research, think about how you are going to create your own logo. You could pay a graphic designer to design it, as long as you've budgeted for it in your business plan. You could also try designing your logo yourself.

FIRST READING

If you have not budgeted for a graphic designer, what other option do you have for creating a logo?

CLOSE READING

In your own words, summarize the reasons why you need a good logo.

How to Design Your Own Logo

THINGS YOU WILL NEED

- a notebook or some blank paper
- a pencil
- an eraser
- a scanner, computer, computer software, and a printer (optional)

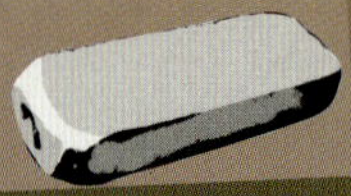

Procedure

STEP 1

Start with some rough thumbnail concepts in a notebook or on a blank sheet of paper. Try to get as many different looks as you can. You can refine your ideas on a computer in step 4. Don't forget, a logo can be just text, or just graphics, or a combination of text and graphics.

STEP 2

Decide which concepts are working the best, revising and refining as you go.

STEP 3

Narrow down your choice to the one or two best concepts. Ask yourself:

- Do these concepts reflect my business? **yes/no**
- Are the concepts legible? **yes/no**
- Can they be reproduced easily in any size, on a wide variety of materials? **yes/no**

If all answers are yes, you can move on to the next step.

STEP 4

At this stage, you can scan in your two best choices and start working with them on a computer.

STEP 5

Using a vector-based computer program, trace your logos. Refine and neaten them.

STEP 6

Try using different fonts and experimenting with different sizes and colors. Print out your logos. How do they look on paper?

STEP 7

Get some feedback on your logos. Which logo got the best response? Does it need refining?

STEP 8

You can try adding different computer effects, such as lighting effects, 2D, and 3D. Just remember that less is more.

STEP 9

Once you've got your final logo done, you can use it on anything: company stationery, T-shirts, T-shirt labels, packaging, signs, Web sites, posters, etc.

FIRST READING

If you are not an experienced artist, how can you get your logo to look the way you want it to?

The Basics of Stationery Design

Have you ever seen a pamphlet or received a letter or a business card that had a tacky, amateurish look? Was it badly designed, photocopied, poorly printed, or all three? What did it tell you about the business behind it? What kind of an impression did it leave on you?

Creating the "right" stationery for your business is almost as important as getting the look of your logo right. Don't be tempted to cut corners by skimping on design or using shoddy materials for your office stationery. It's your one chance to make a lasting impression on your future clients and customers. Most important, it will reinforce your identity and help create opportunities for your business.

Some of the Rules of Stationery Design

1. **Make sure it is eye-catching. First impressions count.**
2. **Keep your logo consistent on the different types of stationery.**
3. **When choosing fonts for different stationery items**
   - Keep the colors consistent and complimentary.
   - Choose a font size that is easily legible.
4. **When choosing paper for different stationery items**
   - Select paper colors that are consistent and will complement your logo.
   - Use high-quality paper.
   - Keep in mind that paper comes in different weights and sizes, so try to ensure the most economical use of whichever paper you choose.
5. **When choosing ink colors for different stationery items**
   - Select colors that are consistent and will complement your logo.
   - Choose colors that are easily legible.

There are many types of stationery, and they all have a different function. What types of business stationery will you need? What can you afford?

- business cards
- envelopes
- invoices
- purchase orders
- brochures
- letterheads
- comment cards
- receipts
- pamphlets
- catalogues
- media releases

Most businesses include important information on their stationery, such as:

- the name of their company
- a tag line briefly stating what their business does
- address details
- telephone numbers (landline and mobile) and fax numbers
- email address
- Web site address (if they have one)

What information will you be putting on your stationery?

The design and printing of business stationery can be expensive and really blow the budget. If you're worried about cost, there are plenty of stores and paper-supply companies out there where you can buy coordinated paper products at a reasonable cost.

With a bit of creative ingenuity, patience, and homework, you could try producing your own stationery. Before you start, do your research and collect as many samples as possible. Business stationery comes in a variety of finishes, shapes, sizes, and colors.

CLOSE READING

What are the most important rules for designing stationery?

How to Design Your Own Stationery

DESIGNING BUSINESS CARDS

Hand out a little piece of yourself by creating your very own business cards.

YOU WILL NEED

- notebook or blank paper
- pencil
- eraser
- scanner, computer, computer software, and printer
- business card stock or plain card stock
- metal ruler
- craft or cutting knife

STEP 1

In a notebook or on a blank sheet of paper, make some rough sketches of how you want your business card to look. Try variations in portrait and landscape formats.

STEP 2

Scan in your two best choices and start working with them on a computer.

✱ TIP: Business cards come in many different sizes and shapes. The standard size is 3.5 inches wide by 2 inches tall. Most computer software packages come with templates for setting up business cards.

STEP 3

Experiment with your logo and fonts in different sizes and colors. Don't forget to include all your important business information.

STEP 4

Print out your two favorite options and cut them out. How do they look on paper? Get some feedback. Which card got the best response? Does it need refining?

STEP 5

Once you've got your final look figured out, print your cards on business card stock or plain card stock and cut them out neatly.

STEP 6

If you want a special finish for your business cards (such as embossing, rounded corners, or foiling), you will need to take them to a professional printer.

Warning: Budget Alert!

FIRST READING

What is the standard size for a business card?

DESIGNING CLOTHING TAGS

With some clever planning, you could adapt the design of your business card to make a clothing tag for your T-shirts. Print them all together to make economical use of paper.

STEP 1

Repeat step 1 of Designing Business Cards. You could even use the same size as your business card.

STEP 2

Scan in your two best choices and start working with them on a computer.

STEP 3

Be sure to include your logo and space for the size and price of your T-shirt. Think about other important information you should include.

STEP 4

Follow steps 4 through 6 of Designing Business Cards.

FIRST READING

What is the purpose of a clothing tag?

The Basics of Setting Up a T-shirt Company

Before you think about designing your own T-shirts—or maybe even starting your own T-shirt business—you need to do some research. Check out the Internet. It's a never-ending source of online stores, T-shirt suppliers, and T-shirt ranking Web sites. Other great research sources are magazines, catalogues, stores, and trade shows.

Before you get started, ask yourself the following hard questions. (You will probably have thought about them for your business plan anyway.)

1. **What's happening in the current market?**
   - what's new, what's not
   - what's in style
   - what's the cost of T-shirts in the market
2. **Who is your target audience/market?**
   - kids
   - young adults
   - adults
3. **Is there a gap in the market for your T-shirts?**
4. **How do you intend to promote and sell your T-shirts?**

Having a clear plan of attack will give you an edge over your competitors and bring back customers time after time. Most important, it will make you money!

FIRST READING

What are some good resources for researching your T-shirt design?

The Basics of T-shirt Design and Printing

Designing and producing T-shirts can seem like a daunting and impossible task. Almost every man and his dog has their own T-shirt company, producing T-shirts by the thousands. However, if you're willing to put in the hard work and use your creativity, designing your own T-shirts can be exciting and a whole lot of fun.

Here are two things to keep in mind before getting started.

THEME

What focus or theme would you like your T-shirts to have?

- sport, urban, elegant, vintage, skater, novelty, political, etc.

STYLE

What style would you like your T-shirts to have?

- long-sleeved, short-sleeved, sleeveless, hoodie, sweatshirt, tank top, etc.
- round neck, V-neck, crew neck, collared, cuffed, etc.
- color—T-shirts come in a variety of colors, and each can be in a single color or multicolored
- fabric—T-shirts come in a variety of fabrics and fabric weights

CLOSE READING

Reread the four questions on page 12. Why does the author characterize these as "hard questions"?

FINISH

- print finish—T-shirts can be printed on the front, back, sleeves, or a combination
- print methods—there are many ways to apply designs to T-shirts, including embroidery, fabric painting, stencilling using spray paints, iron-on or heat transfers, silk screenprinting, etc.

Don't forget quality! A good-quality T-shirt that is well printed will last a lifetime. Nobody wants to buy or wear a T-shirt that fits badly or is made of substandard fabric. The last thing you want is for it to shrink, have the colors run, or for your design to crack or peel off after the first wash.

Start off slowly, test your product, and watch your budget. T-shirt design and printing can be expensive or inexpensive, depending on how you choose to get your shirts produced.

FIRST READING

Why should you make sure your T-shirt is made from good quality fabric?

TIP: The Internet is a great resource for finding places to print and purchase good-quality blank T-shirts at reasonable prices. Plus, you will find a huge variety of colors, shapes, and styles.

How to Design Your Own T-shirt

Using Stencil Design

Creating your own stencil can be done in many different ways. You can draw it freehand on paper or create it using a graphics program on a computer. If you can't draw, various specialty stores sell stencil patterns. To help you get started, flip through magazines and check out the Internet.

The Basics of Stencil Design

Things You Need

- couple of designs/shapes or patterns you like
- fine-point permanent marker with black ink
- few sheets of durable, thickish, transparent plastic (A4 or A3 size, depending on what size your stencil is)
- few old pieces of clean, unbent cardboard
- craft/cutting knife
- rubber gloves and face mask
- sticky tape
- can of black fabric spray paint
- few heavy objects (such as rocks or bricks)

Procedure

one

Select a design/shape or a pattern you want to trace. If you can draw freehand, you won't need a pattern. Ensure that your design has disconnected parts (parts that are not linked).

two

Take a sheet of plastic and place it over the design you want to trace. With sticky tape, firmly stick down both the image you want to trace and the clear plastic sheet.

three

Using a fine-point permanent marker, trace your image carefully, first as an outline. Take your time.

four

When you have finished tracing your design, fill in/color in the outlines of the design. This will give you a good idea of what your stencil design will look like when it's on your finished product.

FIRST READING

Why does Step 8 advise you to take your work outside?

five

Carefully lift the plastic sheet that has your finished design on it, and stick it down onto a piece of cardboard.

six

It's time to cut out your stencil. Using a craft/cutting knife, carefully cut along the lines of your design. Take your time and try to do it neatly. You don't want to mess it up or cut yourself.

seven

Once you have finished, get a clean sheet of cardboard—one big enough to fit your plastic stencil over. With tape, stick down your newly cut-out stencil onto the cardboard.

eight

Take your work outside. Find a place that is not too dusty or too windy. With a few heavy bricks/rocks, anchor the piece of cardboard holding your plastic stencil.

nine Put on your rubber gloves and face mask. Give the can of fabric spray paint a really good shake. Hold the can at a 45-degree angle about 10 inches away from your plastic stencil. Spray evenly over your stencil until you feel there is enough paint coverage.

*** TIP:** Don't spray too much. You don't want the paint to bleed or smudge under the plastic stencil.

ten

Wait about five minutes to make sure the spray paint has dried.

eleven

Lift the plastic stencil carefully away from the piece of cardboard. Check out the results. Keep practicing until you feel ready to try stencilling on a T-shirt.

CLOSE READING

How would you summarize the stencil design procedure in your own words?

Something Different

You could always try a different approach with your stencil.

Procedure

1 

Take the shape that was left over when you cut out your stencil.

2 Break off a few pieces of sticky tape and fold them into circles, sticky side facing out (like double-sided tape). With these bits of tape, stick the cut-out shape down onto a clean piece of cardboard.

3 Repeat step 8 from previous instructions.

4 Put on your rubber gloves and face mask. Shake the can of fabric spray paint. Hold the can at a 45-degree angle about 10 inches away from your cut-out shape. Spray a gentle layer of paint over your cut-out shape until it forms an outline of the shape.

5 

Wait about five minutes to make sure the spray paint has dried.

6 

Lift the cut-out shape carefully away from the piece of cardboard. Check out the results. It's a different approach to stencilling!

How to Stencil Your Own T-shirt

STUFF YOU WILL NEED

- the design you want to create a stencil of
- blank, white T-shirt
- few old pieces of cardboard (bigger than your stencil and small enough to fit inside your T-shirt)
- craft/cutting knife
- rubber gloves and face mask
- can of black fabric spray paint
- computer, computer software, and a printer
- few heavy objects (such as rocks or bricks)

STEPS

STEP 1

Option 1: Using a computer printer, print your design onto thick card.

Option 2: Take a sheet of plastic and place it over the design you want to trace. With sticky tape, firmly stick down both the image you want to trace and the clear plastic sheet.

STEP 2

Option 1: Using a craft/cutting knife, cut along the black bits of your design. Do it carefully.

Option 2: Follow steps 3, 4, 5, and 6 on pages 15 and 16, and then skip to step 3 (below).

STEP 3

Take your blank T-shirt, stencil, gloves, and spray paint into a room where messing around with spray paint won't get you into trouble, or take them outside. Find a calm, clean spot.
Spread your T-shirt on a piece of cardboard. Insert a piece of cardboard inside the T-shirt, between the front and the back.

CLOSE READING

Think about the way in which the author presents instructions. Are they easy to follow? Why or why not?

STEP 4

Ensure your T-shirt is positioned so that it is flat, with no wrinkles or folds. Place your stencil on top of the T-shirt, making sure you are happy with the way it is positioned.

STEP 5

Anchor the stencil down so it does not move or blow away. Place some pieces of cardboard over the edges of your stencil and completely cover any part of your T-shirt that you don't want sprayed with spray paint.

*** TIP:** If you are using text in your stencil, be sure to create it separately. You will need to mirror it when spraying your T-shirt.

STEP 6

Put on your rubber gloves and face mask. Spray the paint evenly over your stencil until you feel there is enough paint coverage.

STEP 7

Wait about five minutes to make sure the spray paint has dried.

STEP 8

Carefully lift the stencil. Check out the results—your very own one-off, custom-made T-shirt.

Get some feedback from friends and family. Do they like it? Is there anything they would change? Would they pay money for your T-shirt? Do they honestly think your T-shirt could sell?

When you're ready, create a few more of your custom-made T-shirts, using different colors, sizes, and styles of T-shirt and different colors of spray paint. This way, you have some merchandise samples to show potential customers. First you need to package them to get that professional look.

The Basics of Package Design

In today's world, to make your product stand out from the menagerie of competing products, you need to have an "edge" when it comes to packaging. Everywhere you look, products are covered or protected by some form of packaging.

Typically, packaging

- comes in many shapes and sizes.
- is made from a diverse range of materials, such as glass, paper (cartons, cardboard, molded fiber), plastic (bags, film, PVC), or metals (tin, aluminium, foil).
- is used in all types of industries, such as technology, food and beverages, fashion and beauty, medicine, books and media, and office and art supplies.
- has many functions, including protection, safety and hygiene, ease of identification, informing and attracting, marketing, and selling.

FIRST READING

What should be the main focus of your packaging?

Here are a few tips to help you create effective packaging.

- Focus your packaging on your specific target audience.
- Try to create packaging that is reusable and recyclable.
- Choose the right material for your packaging. Consider durability, weight, formability, color, texture, touch and feel, etc.
- Make an innovative, unique design the main focus of your packaging.
- Ensure your packaging has that little something extra or an element of fun.
- Use color or metallic finishes in your packaging and labeling. If your budget allows it, sandwich printing on labeling is an effective way to give your customers more information about you.

While you're just finding your feet in the business world, getting your packaging figured out in the conventional way can really drain your bank account.

The good news is that there are other clever ways to create eye-catching packaging at a reasonable cost or even no cost. Have a look around you and try to think outside the square. Always remember, your choice of packaging can determine the success of your product.

CLOSE READING

What are the main characteristics of typical packaging?

How to Design Your Own Package

YOU WILL NEED

- old piece of cardboard (for practicing)
- old cardboard boxes or sheets of cardboard (clean if possible and not too thick)
- pencil
- fine-pointed colored markers or pens in red, blue, green, and black
- eraser
- cutting knife and scissors
- glue
- L-shaped metal ruler
- protractor

* TIP: Reduce, reuse, and recycle

PRACTICING SCORING AND FOLDING

1 Practice your scoring and folding techniques on an old piece of cardboard. With your pencil and ruler, draw some random straight lines.

2 With your scissors, score along a pencil line by gently running the tip of the scissor blade along it. Try scoring some more lines, using slightly different pressure each time.

3 Gently fold the cardboard along the different scored lines. Try to remember which scored line worked the best.

* TIP: Don't score too hard. You don't want to cut right through the cardboard.

Creating Your Package

IMPORTANT NOTE

Before you start, measure the thickness of your cardboard. When drawing the different colored lines to create your package, you will need to offset your score lines by the thickness of your cardboard in some places, to allow your package to be folded neatly.

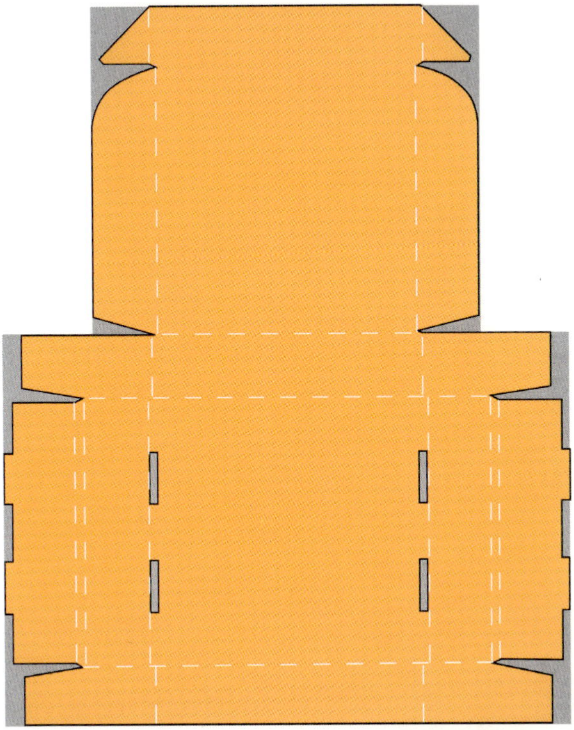

1 Cut out a rectangle of cardboard, 18 in x 14.33 in. Then draw this shape onto the cardboard.

2 Take your red marker and L-shaped metal ruler and mark out lines as shown in red. Your lines need to be absolutely straight.

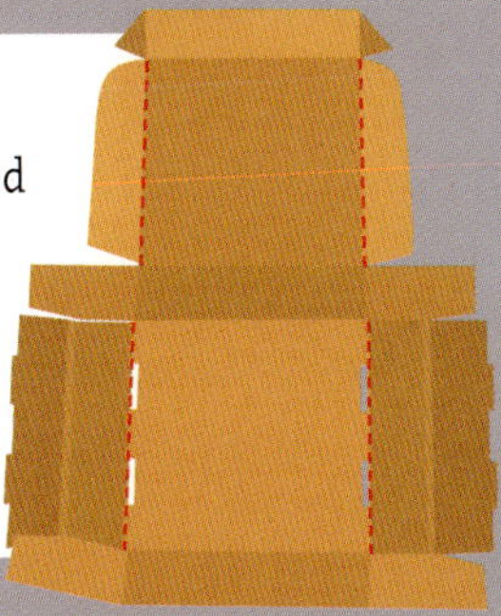

3 Mark out four small rectangles as shown in blue.

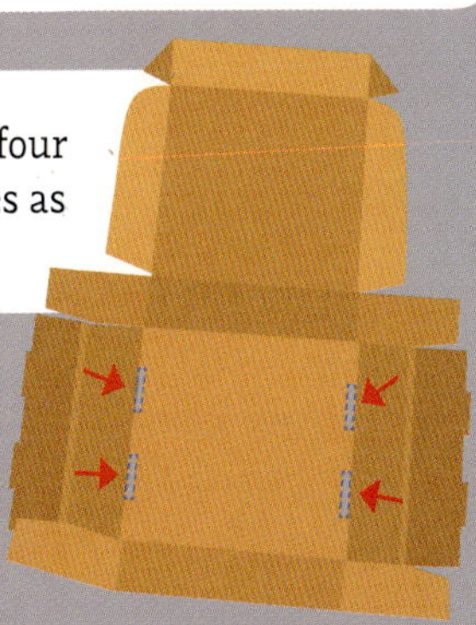

4 With a craft/cutting knife, carefully cut out the blue rectangle holes.

5 Mark out the tabs as shown, and cut them out. Be sure the tabs are in the same position as your cut-out rectangles.

FIRST READING

What is the purpose of measuring the cardboard's thickness?

6 Next, grab your green marker and L-shaped metal ruler and mark out lines as shown in green.

7 With your black marker and L-shaped metal ruler, mark out lines as shown in black.

8 Score all the lines carefully with your scissors. Carefully fold the cardboard inwards along all your scored lines to create neat fold lines.

9 With your red marker and L-shaped metal ruler, mark out lines as shown in dotted lines.

10 Score and fold these lines inward.

11 With your cutting knife, cut little wedges in the cardboard as shown.

12 With a pencil, lightly draw two circles 25.5 inches in diameter. Cut along the outer edge on both sides of your package to get rounded corners.

13 Fold along all the lines again to make sure they fold in neatly and easily.

14 Fold the parts marked "A" upward and inward as shown.

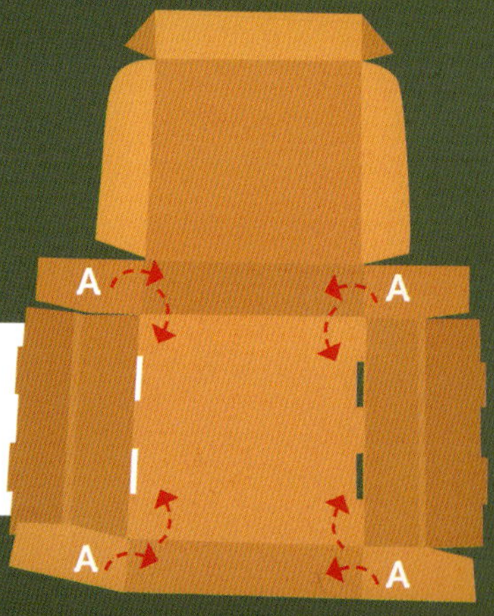

15 Next, fold the parts marked "B" so they fold over or cover the parts marked "A." Slot or tuck the tabs into your cut-out rectangle holes.

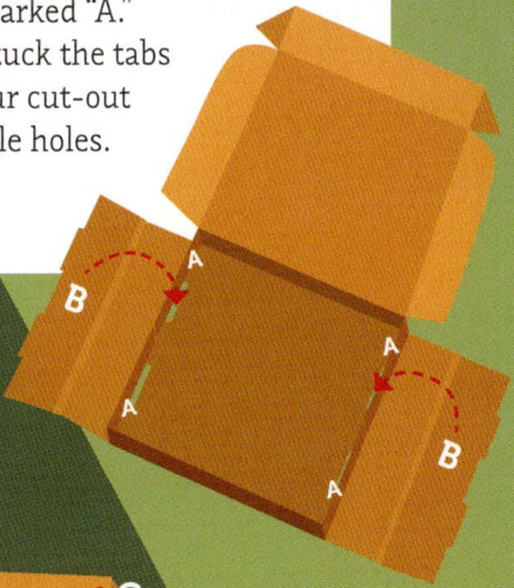

16 You should now see a neat square base to your box.

17 Fold the parts marked "C" inward, as shown, and close the lid down. You should now have a complete box with a lid that is closed.

18 Fold the flaps marked "C" down, and slot them into the little gaps down the side of the bottom of your box.

Decorating Your Package

It is best to decorate your package after you have cut it out and scored it. Different decoration techniques include

- spray-painting the entire package in a solid color and sticking one of your business cards somewhere prominent,
- keeping your package *au naturel* to get that organic look (the cardboard needs to be free of ugly marks, and don't forget your business card),
- spray-painting and then stencilling your package with your logo, and
- creating a label and sticking that on the top or on the sides of your package.

When you've finished decorating it, you can slot your neatly folded T-shirt into your very own custom-made package. Don't forget that the clothing tag should be easily visible when you open the box.

FIRST READING

When is it best to decorate your package?

Another Cost-effective and Clever Packaging Alternative

YOU WILL NEED

- recycled black plastic ice-cream tubs with lids (washed/clean and big enough to fit a T-shirt in)
- can of spray paint (black)
- computer, computer graphics software, and a printer (optional)
- white printer-compatible adhesive labels

PROCEDURE

1 First you need to get rid of any old wording/marketing on the ice-cream tub. You can either wash it off or spray-paint over it.

2 Now decide how you are going to brand your package. You could stencil it or create labels for it. Don't forget to wait until all the paint is completely dry before moving on to the next step.

3 Fold your T-shirt into a neat little roll so that it fits comfortably into the ice-cream tub. Place the clothing tag so that it faces up when you seal the package.

4 Print your logo and any other relevant information on the adhesive labels. You can do this yourself or at a print store. Finally, stick the labels on your packages.

FIRST READING

What should you print on the adhesive labels?

What Next?

Once you have your business stationery, T-shirt samples, and packaging completed, it's time to start selling. It's time for Sk8r Jam Apparel to start making you some money.

You can do this in several ways:

- Show your samples to friends and family and ask them for orders.
- You could display your shirts at skate competitions, flea markets, and craft shows, and either sell them (if you have enough made) or take orders.
- You could create some flyers and stick them up at your local skate park, school, in local stores, or in various places in your neighborhood. (Make sure you get permission first.)
- You could register your designs on the Internet and take orders from there.
- You could create a page on one of the many social networks on the Internet, and use it to get free advertising and to generate interest in your T-shirts.
- When your budget allows, you could create your very own Web site and sell directly to your market.

Remember, take it slowly, and as your parents keep telling you: "Rome wasn't built in a day." Yeah, right!

CLOSE READING

What does the quote in the last paragraph mean? Why is this an effective conclusion to the book?

THINK ABOUT THE TEXT

MAKING CONNECTIONS

Which of the following connections can you make to the instructions presented in *Design It, Edition 2*?

TEXT TO SELF

- Visualizing the end product
- Listening to others
- Thinking about sequence and being able to think logically
- Taking responsible risks
- Being able to question and problem-solve
- Being organized and planning ahead
- Understanding and following procedures
- Being open to trying things out instead of just doing ordinary stuff
- Thinking creatively

TEXT TO TEXT/MEDIA

Talk about other procedural texts you may have read or seen that have similar features. Compare the texts.

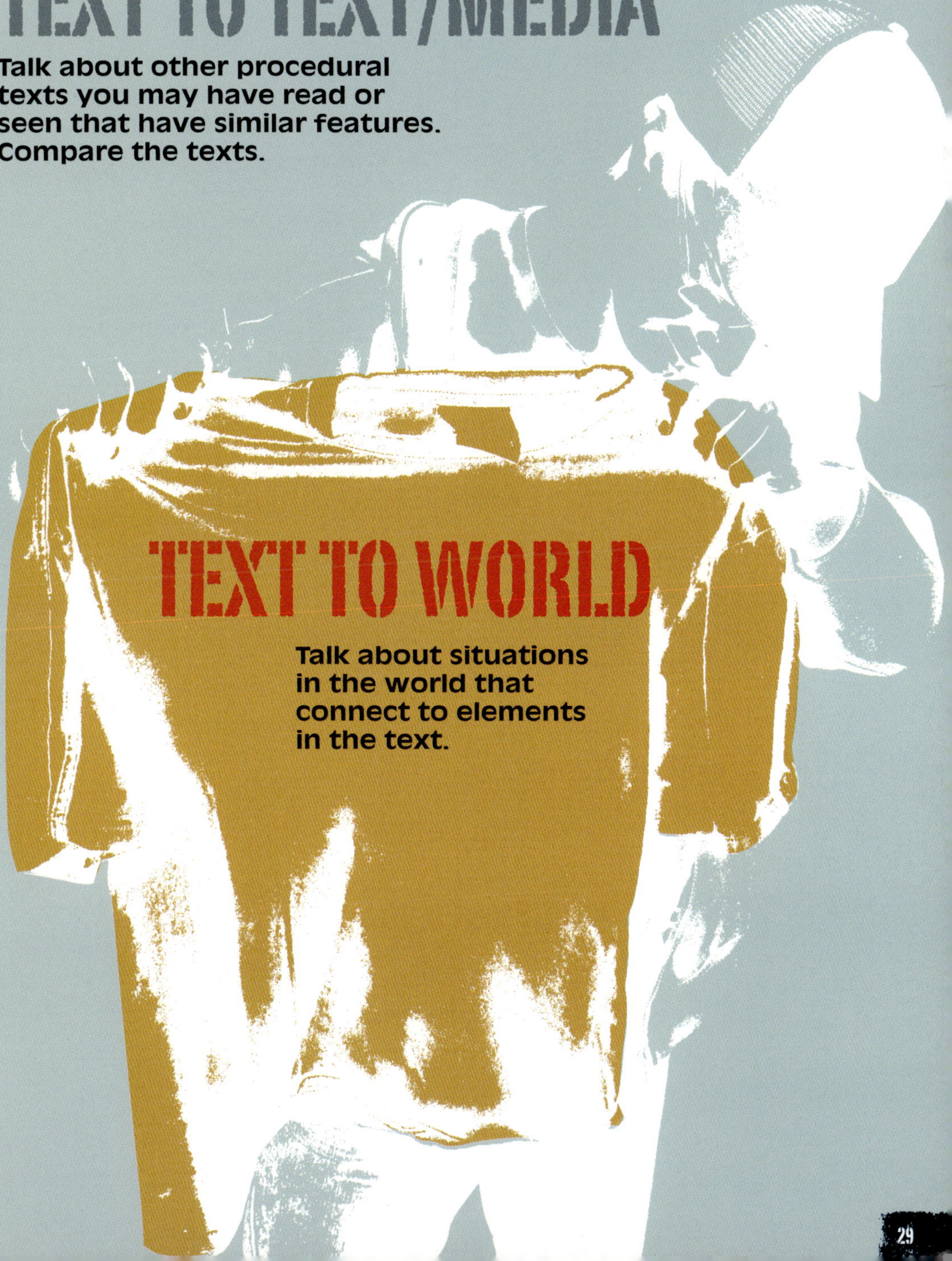

TEXT TO WORLD

Talk about situations in the world that connect to elements in the text.

PLANNING A PROCEDURAL TEXT

THINK ABOUT

the audience you want to target. Consider the age group and how much general knowledge they have of the subject.

THINK ABOUT

the purpose of the instructions. Are they designed to communicate how to make something, use something, or learn a new skill?

THINK ABOUT

the language you will use. Is formal, technical, scientific, conversational, or simple, precise language appropriate for your reader?

THINK ABOUT

the information the reader will need to carry out the procedures.

THINK ABOUT

a sequence that will make sense. Which should come first, next, and last?

How to Make → Statement of Goal → Materials → Steps in Order

How to Do → Statement of Goal → Steps in Order

How to Use → Materials → Steps in Order

THINK ABOUT

how you can make your procedural text clear and easy to follow.

- Use headings and subheadings to organize information
- Use diagrams, photographs, illustrations, maps, cross-sections
- Use numbered steps, bullet points, arrows, captions, labels
- Use lists

WRITING A PROCEDURAL TEXT

HAVE YOU . . .

- provided a context, a goal, or aims for your instructions?
- avoided straying from the topic or purpose?
- provided accurate and reliable information?
- included action verbs, such as: trace, sketch, score, remove, cover, make, cut . . .
- used clear, concise language that is easy to follow?
- used words that indicate sequence, such as: next, after, then, before . . .
- written in the present tense or future tense?
- included lists of materials or ingredients needed?
- included visual elements that clarify the text, such as: headings, subheadings, drawings, schematic diagrams, maps, photographs, labels, illustrations, bullets, numbers, arrows, captions . . .
- included rules or guidelines?

Do you need to change, add, or delete anything to improve your procedural text?

DON'T FORGET TO REVISIT YOUR WRITING!